D1165633

20 Questions: Physical Science

What Do You Know About Simple Machines?

Tilda Monroe

PowerKiDS press
New York

Published in 2011 by The Rosen Publishing Group, Inc.
29 East 21st Street, New York, NY 10010

First Edition

Editor: Amelie von Zumbusch
Book Design: Kate Laczynski
Layout Design: Ashley Burrell
Photo Researcher: Jessica Gerweck

Photo Credits: Cover John Howard/Getty Images; pp. 5, 6, 7, 8, 9, 10, 11(bottom), 13, 15, 16, 18, 19, 20, 22 Shutterstock.com; p. 11 (top) Yellow Dog Productions/Getty Images; p. 12 (left) © www.iStockphoto.com/Luxian; p. 12 (right) © www.iStockphoto.com/Bruce Turner; p. 14 © www.iStockphoto.com/Todd Aarnes; p. 17 (top) © www.iStockphoto.com/Digitalskillet; p.17 (bottom) © www.iStockphoto.com/Simon Podgorsek; p. 21 Time & Life Pictures/Getty Images.

Library of Congress Cataloging-in-Publication Data

Monroe, Tilda.
What do you know about simple machines? / Tilda Monroe. — 1st ed.
p. cm. — (20 questions. Physical science)
Includes index.
ISBN 978-1-4488-0674-4 (library binding) — ISBN 978-1-4488-1257-8 (pbk.) — ISBN 978-1-4488-1258-5 (6-pack)
1. Simple machines—Juvenile literature. I. Title.
TJ147.M58 2011
621.8—dc22

2010002557

Manufactured in the United States of America

CPSIA Compliance Information: Batch #WS10PK: For Further Information contact Rosen Publishing, New York, New York at 1-800-237-9932

Contents

Simple yet Helpful 4
1. What is work? 6
2. How common are simple machines? 7
3. What is a lever? 8
4. What does a lever do? 8
5. Is a seesaw a lever? 9
6. Are the wheels on my bike a simple machine? 10
7. How do we use wheels and axles? 11
8. What is a pulley? 12
9. How does it work? 13
10. Why do we need pulleys? 13
11. Is a ramp a simple machine? 14
12. What kind of work does an inclined plane help us do? 15
13. Are there other kinds of inclined planes? 16
14. Is a doorstop a wedge? 16
15. What are some other wedges? 17
16. What is a screw? 18
17. How does a screw work? 19
18. Are there other simple kinds of machines? 20
19. How long have people been using simple machines? 21
20. Do we still need simple machines today? 22
Glossary 23
Index and Web Sites 24

Simple yet Helpful

A long time ago, when our clothes got dirty, we had to wash them by hand. This work took a lot of **energy**. Today we have washing machines to wash our clothes. Machines make our lives easier!

Some machines have many parts. For example, the cars, buses, and trains that take us where we need to go have lots of parts. Machines with many parts are called compound machines or complex machines. Other machines are made of just a few parts. These are called simple machines. Like other machines, these machines make our lives easier. Levers, pulleys, and wedges are just a few kinds of simple machines.

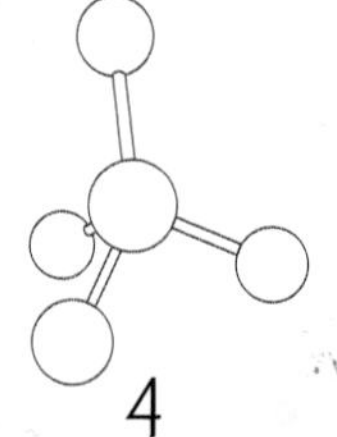

These kids are riding bicycles. Have you ever ridden a bicycle? A bicycle is a complex machine. It uses several simple machines, such as pulleys, wheels and axles, and levers.

1. What is work?

Scientists define work as the force that acts on an object so that it can be moved some distance. When we push, pull, and lift objects, we are doing work. Over time, people and some other animals have found that using tools makes work easier. A shovel helps us dig in the earth. A flat board can be used to slide a heavy box from the ground to a shelf. The most basic kinds of tools that help us do work are simple machines.

This boy is digging a hole with a shovel. Shovels are useful tools. Think how much harder it would be to dig a hole using only your hands!

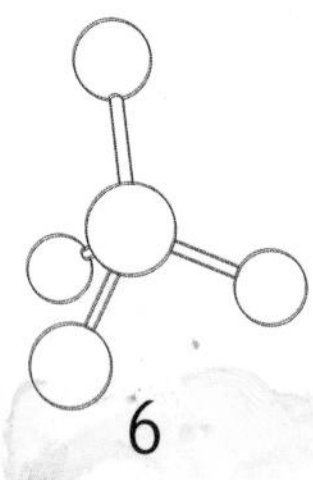

2. How common are simple machines?

Simple machines are very common. **Construction** workers and movers use them every day. The basic simple machines are levers, wheels and axles, pulleys, inclined planes, wedges, and screws.

A waterwheel, such as this one, is one example of a wheel and axle. In the past, people often used waterwheels to power mills.

This is an oil pump jack. It is used to draw oil out of the ground. It uses a lever and several pulleys.

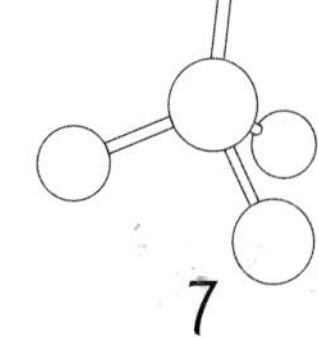

3. What is a lever?

A lever is a simple machine. It is made up of an object that moves up and down on a **fulcrum**. The fulcrum is also known as a pivot. It can be in the center of the lever, at one end, or anywhere in between.

Tower cranes, such as this one, are used in construction. The long, sideways part of the crane is a lever. Its fulcrum is the point where it meets the upright part of the crane.

4. What does a lever do?

Levers make it easier to lift loads. Let's say there is a load on one end of a lever. If force is applied to the other end, the load can be easily lifted and lowered.

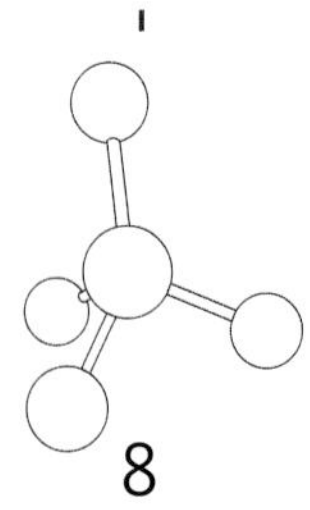

On a seesaw, it is easy for a smaller kid to lift a larger kid off the ground. It would be much harder to do so with no help from a simple machine.

5. Is a seesaw a lever?

Yes, seesaws are levers. Even if you ride a seesaw with an adult, you can lift the other person up without a lot of work. Scissors are another kind of lever. The back part of a hammer, which is used to pull out nails, is a lever, too.

The man on the left is using a crowbar to lift up some boards. The crowbar is acting as a lever. Its fulcrum is at the end under the boards.

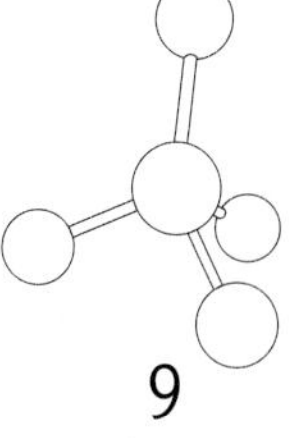

6. Are the wheels on my bike a simple machine?

Yes, a bike wheel is an example of a wheel and axle. As you may know, a wheel is a round object that rolls easily. An axle is a rod that is fixed to the center of a wheel. The wheel spins if you turn the axle, and the axle spins if you turn the wheel. A bicycle wheel turns and moves you forward when your pedaling spins its axle.

When you are pedaling a bicycle, the wheel that your pedaling makes turn is the back wheel. This is what powers the bike. The front wheel spins around but does not move you forward.

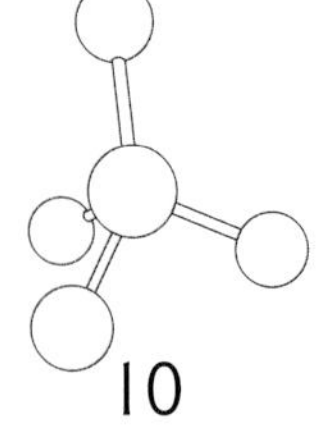

7. How do we use wheels and axles?

You might not guess it, but doorknobs, screwdrivers, and **ceiling** fans are wheels and axles, too. Cars and trucks move thanks to wheels and axles. Without wheels and axles, a bus could never move from one stop to the next!

When you turn a doorknob, it turns the narrow axle inside. It takes less force to turn the outside of a wheel than it does to turn the axle. This makes it easier to open the door.

The wheel in a wheel and axle does not always look like a circle. For example, wind turbines, such as those below, are wheels and axles.

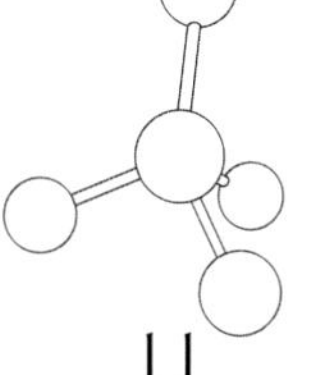

8. What is a pulley?

A pulley is a simple machine that helps us lift heavy objects. The most basic pulleys are just a rope or cable that goes around a wheel and axle.

The cover on this well can be lifted using a pulley. It is a lot easier to lift the cover by pulling down on the rope than it would be to pull up the well cover.

Here, a pulley is being used to lift the sail on a sailboat. Pulleys are used a lot on sailboats.

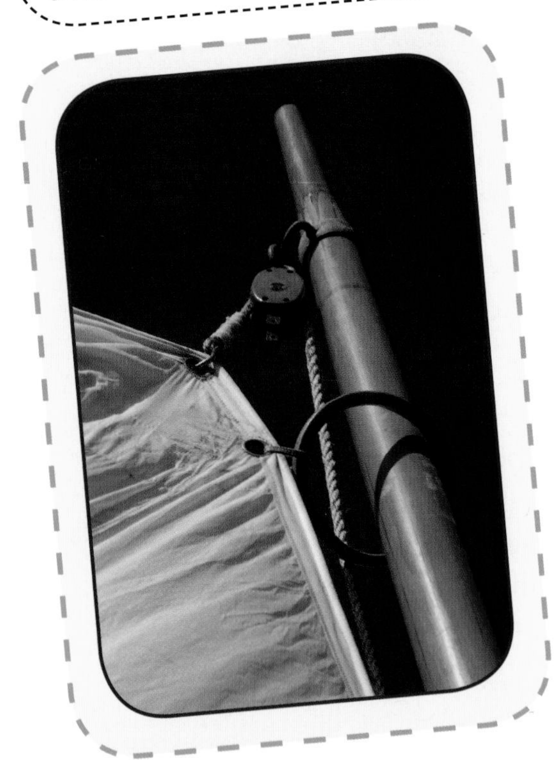

This is a block and tackle. A block and tackle is a group of pulleys that are on the same rope. The more pulleys you use, the less force you need to move something.

9. How does it work?

A pulley is often fixed to a ceiling or some other high place. The wheel has a groove, or path through which the rope goes. This keeps the rope from slipping. The rope may go through one or more pulley wheels. A person can pull on the free end of the rope and lift a heavy object.

10. Why do we need pulleys?

Pulleys are used in construction, when heavy building **materials** need to be lifted or moved. Pulleys are also helpful on flagpoles. A pulley lets you raise or lower a flag while standing on the ground.

11. Is a ramp a simple machine?

A ramp is a kind of simple machine called an inclined plane. An inclined plane is a flat **surface** that is on a slant. When something is on a slant, it means one end is higher than the other end.

This man is using a ramp to move his boat from his truck into the water. Ramps are often used to put small boats into the water.

12. What kind of work does an inclined plane help us do?

Inclined planes, such as ramps, make it easier to bring a load from one height to another.

The ramp this man is using to put a dryer into a moving van is somewhat steep. The steeper a ramp is, the more force it takes to move something up it.

Think about lifting your bike from the ground to the back of a moving truck. It would take less work to push the bike up a ramp into the back of the truck. The distance you have to move your bike would be greater, but the effort you have to use would be less.

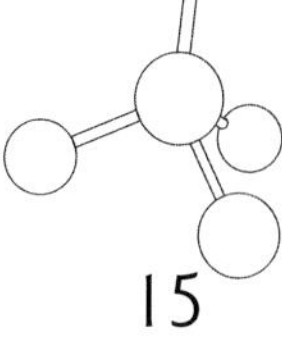

13. Are there other kinds of inclined planes?

A wedge is made from two inclined planes put back-to-back. It is shaped like a triangle. People use wedges to **split** wood. They hold the wedge, with the point facing down, on the wood. Then they hit the wedge with a hammer. The wood splits where it meets the wedge's point. Our front teeth are like wedges, too. They let us cut through food.

A wooden doorstop, such as this one, is one of the simplest examples of a wedge.

14. Is a doorstop a wedge?

Yes, it is. A doorstop slides under a door and keeps it from opening. It does a lot of work for something that just sits on the ground!

This woman is using a knife to cut up vegetables. Knives are very thin wedges.

15. What are some other wedges?

Lots of tools, such as **chisels**, knives, and axes, are wedges. The **hulls** of many boats are also wedges. Their pointed shapes let these boats cut through the water.

Axes are often used to cut wood. Cutting wood with an ax is a lot like cutting wood with a wedge and a hammer. However, on an ax, the wedge and the hammer are the same thing!

16. What is a screw?

It may seem hard to believe, but a screw is a kind of inclined plane. Picture a ramp that goes around a rod. That is a screw! The screw must move to work, though.

If you look closely at this picture of a screw, you can see that a screw really is an inclined plane that curls around.

Corkscrews, such as this one, are also a kind of screw. In a corkscrew, though, the inclined plane is just wrapped around air!

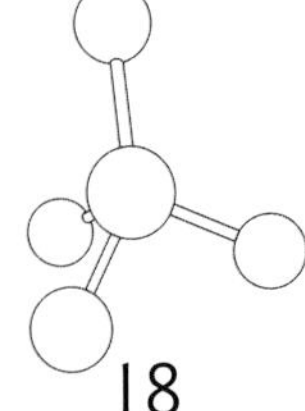

17. How does a screw work?

It takes less force to push something up a ramp than to lift it, right? It also takes less force to twist a screw into a wall than it does to hammer in a nail. Screws are most often used to hold things, such as a wall and a shelf, together. They can also be used to lift things or push things forward. Piano stools, corkscrews, and boat **propellers** all use screws in this way.

Can you see the screw in the snowblower that this man is using? The screw pushes snow up as it turns.

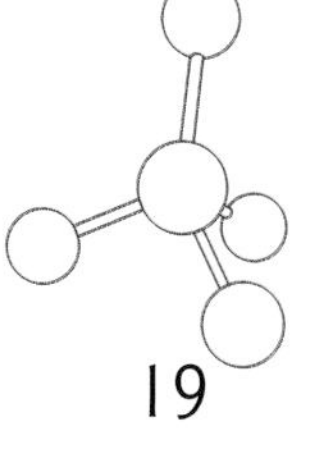

18. Are there other simple kinds of machines?

Yes, there are. These machines build upon the basic simple machines. Gears, or wheels with teeth, are important simple machines. They make bicycles and watches work. **Hinges**, such as those on doors, are a kind of lever.

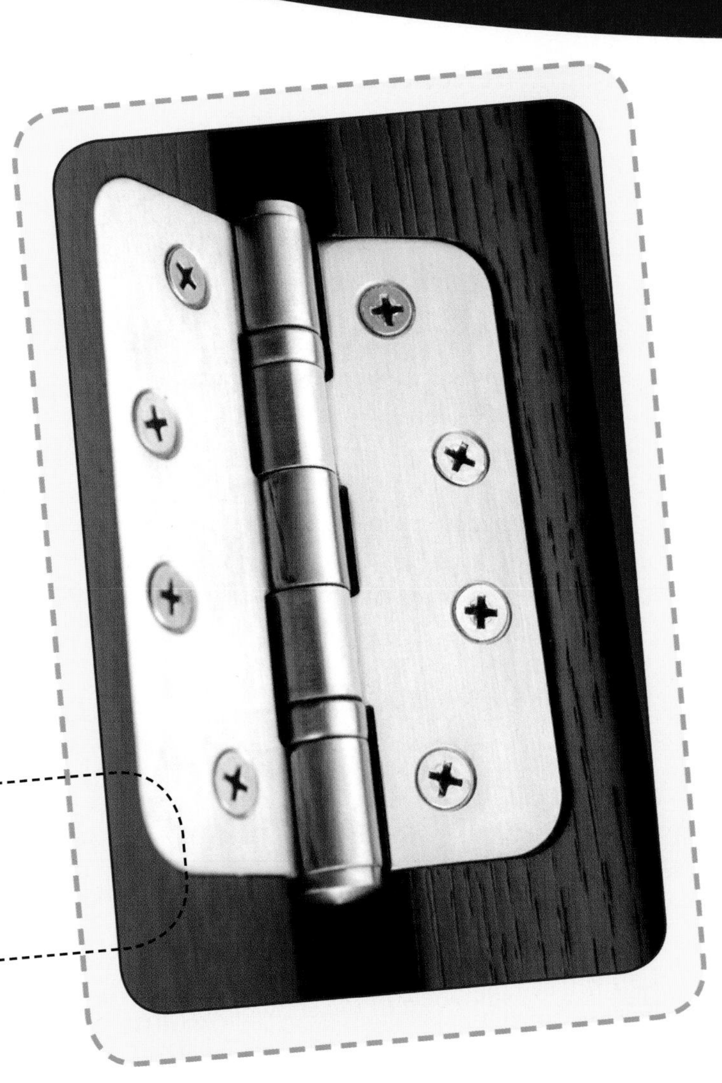

Hinges let people open a door easily. They also make it possible to open a box without having to take the lid all the way off.

19. How long have people been using simple machines?

People have used simple machines for thousands of years. Levers, ramps, and pulleys were used in ancient Egypt to build the Great **Pyramids**. Native Americans who used spears to hunt were using wedges. In the third century BC, the Greek scientist Archimedes invented a way to lift water, called the Archimedes screw. It was used to water crops and to move water out of ships.

This drawing shows an Archimedes screw. As the screw in the pipe is turned, the water inside the pipe moves up and spills out of the top.

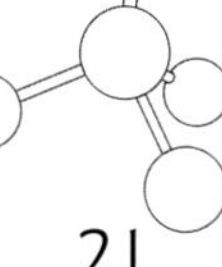

20. Do we still need simple machines today?

Our world is full of machines. Many of them are complex, such as computers and jet engines. However, these complex machines are here thanks to simple machines or the ideas behind them. **Skyscrapers**, bridges, and roads are all built with the help of simple machines. Houses are built with hammers and drills. Metal **girders** are lifted into the sky with pulleys. They may be simple, but these machines are truly important!

Huge cranes, such as this one, are often used in construction. These complex machines use several simple machines, such as pulleys and levers.

Glossary

ceiling (SEE-ling) The inside roof of a room.
chisels (CHIH-zulz) Sharp tools used to cut and shape wood or stone.
construction (kun-STRUK-shun) Having to do with building.
energy (EH-ner-jee) The power to work or to act.
fulcrum (FUL-krum) The point on which a lever moves.
girders (GUR-derz) Long, strong pieces used to hold together buildings and bridges.
hinges (HINJ-ez) Bendable parts.
hulls (HULZ) The frames, or bodies, of ships.
materials (muh-TEER-ee-ulz) What things are made of.
propellers (pruh-PEL-erz) Paddlelike parts on an object that spin to move the object forward.
pyramids (PEER-uh-midz) Huge buildings that held the graves of Egyptian rulers called pharaohs.
scientists (SY-un-tists) People who study the world.
skyscrapers (SKY-skray-perz) Very tall buildings.
split (SPLIT) To break up into parts.
surface (SER-fes) The outside of anything.

Index

B
bus(es), 4, 11

C
cars, 4, 11

D
doorknobs, 11

E
energy, 4

F
fulcrum, 8

G
girders, 22
Great Pyramids, 21

H
hinges, 20
hulls, 17

L
lever(s), 4, 7–9, 20–21

M
materials, 13

P
part(s), 4, 9
people, 6, 9, 13, 16, 21
propellers, 19

S
scientist(s), 6, 21
skyscrapers, 22

T
trains, 4

W
work, 4, 6, 9, 15–16, 20

Web Sites

Due to the changing nature of Internet links, PowerKids Press has developed an online list of Web sites related to the subject of this book. This site is updated regularly. Please use this link to access the list:
www.powerkidslinks.com/quest/sm/